CIVIC VIRTUE
LET'S WORK TOGETHER

THE PURPOSE OF RULES AND LAWS

JOSHUA TURNER

PowerKiDS press.

New York

Published in 2019 by The Rosen Publishing Group, Inc.
29 East 21st Street, New York, NY 10010

First Edition

Editor: Melissa Raé Shofner
Book Design: Tanya Dellaccio

Photo Credits: Cover Wealan Pollard/OJO Images/Getty Images; p. 5 andresr/E+/Getty Images; p. 7 (Capitol Building) MH Anderson Photography/Shutterstock.com; p. 7 (Congress meeting) Chip Somodevilla/Getty Images News/Getty Images; p. 9 Rawpixel.com/Shutterstock.com; p. 11 Ariel Skelley/DigitalVision/Getty Images; p. 13 (White House) Andrea Izzotti/Shutterstock.com; p. 13 (US Capitol) turtix/Shutterstock.com; p. 13 (Supreme Court Building) Diego Grandi/Shutterstock.com; p. 15 (MLK Jr.) Consolidated News Pictures/Hulton Archive/Getty Images; p. 15 Hero Images/Getty Images; p. 17 (signing the Constitution) https://commons.wikimedia.org/wiki/File:Scene_at_the_Signing_of_the_Constitution_of_the_United_States.jpg; p. 17 (US Constitution) https://commons.wikimedia.org/wiki/File:Constitution_of_the_United_States,_page_1.jpg; p. 19 Maskot/Getty Images; p. 21 SAEED KHAN/AFP/Getty Images; p. 22 Kinga/Shutterstock.com.

Cataloging-in-Publication Data

Names: Turner, Joshua.
Title: The purpose of rules and laws / Joshua Turner.
Description: New York : PowerKids Press, 2019. | Series: Civic virtue: let's work together | Includes glossary and index.
Identifiers: LCCN ISBN 9781508166962 (pbk.) | ISBN 9781508166948 (library bound) | ISBN 9781508166979 (6 pack)
Subjects: LCSH: Law–Juvenile literature. | Social norms–Juvenile literature.
Classification: LCC K246.T87 2019 | DDC 340'.1–dc23

Manufactured in the United States of America

CPSIA Compliance Information: Batch #CS18PK: For Further Information contact Rosen Publishing, New York, New York at 1-800-237-9932

CONTENTS

LIFE WITHOUT RULES

What would life be like without rules? Imagine you've just sat down to play a card game with your friends. You deal out the cards to play but realize you don't know what the rules are. How can you play the game?

Pretend you're waiting in line at the movies and someone cuts ahead of you. You want to say something, but there are no rules against cutting in line. Life without rules would be harder than we think.

PEOPLE FORMED SOCIETIES BECAUSE IT MADE LIFE BETTER AND MORE **PREDICTABLE**. IN ORDER TO HAVE GOOD SOCIETIES, PEOPLE NEED RULES AND LAWS.

MANY GREAT THINKERS HAVE LONG WONDERED WHAT THE WORLD WAS LIKE BEFORE SOCIETIES AROSE. THEY BELIEVED A "STATE OF NATURE" EXISTED IN WHICH PEOPLE WERE ABLE TO DO WHAT THEY WANTED ALL THE TIME.

THE DIFFERENCE BETWEEN RULES AND LAWS

Rules and laws keep people safe, maintain peace, and uphold a society's morals and values. Even though they have similar purposes, rules and laws aren't the same. Rules are like guidelines for our behaviors, or actions, while laws are much more **serious**.

Think of the rules in your classroom or home. They're made and **enforced** by people who are close to you to help you become a good person. Laws are created and enforced by governments and police. Laws are harder to make, and breaking them has more serious **consequences**.

IN THE UNITED STATES, LAWS ARE MADE IN THE CAPITOL BUILDING. REPRESENTATIVES FROM ACROSS THE COUNTRY COME TOGETHER TO MAKE LAWS FOR THE GREATER GOOD OF U.S. CITIZENS.

CITIZENS IN ACTION

THE UNITED STATES IS A REPRESENTATIVE DEMOCRACY. THIS MEANS THAT CITIZENS ELECT OFFICIALS TO **REPRESENT** THEM IN GOVERNMENT. THIS ALLOWS CITIZENS TO HAVE A SAY IN THEIR GOVERNMENT, INCLUDING THE MAKING OF LAWS.

WHY WE HAVE RULES

Rules are easier to enforce and easier to change than laws. They're also flexible, which means they can be easily changed to fit different conditions by the people who make them.

Rules allow people such as teachers or parents to have order without having to go through all the steps of passing laws. If teachers had to pass a law every time they wanted to change the way they run their classrooms, nothing would ever get done.

RULES HELP SMALLER GROUPS OF PEOPLE, SUCH AS YOUR FAMILY OR CLASS, UNDERSTAND HOW THEY SHOULD BEHAVE DURING EVERYDAY ACTIVITIES.

THE IMPORTANCE OF LAWS

Laws usually apply to a larger number of people than rules do. They let people in these large groups know what they can and can't do in society. Because laws effect so many people, they take a long time to make and aren't easy to change.

Laws are important because they let people know what behaviors, or ways of acting, are acceptable in society. People know that if they break a law they'll be in trouble and this **encourages** people to act better.

WHO MAKES LAWS?

In the United States, elected officials make laws. These representatives listen to the people, then vote to make laws based on what the people want. It can take a long time for lawmakers to come to an agreement about what a law should say.

Elections allow citizens to vote for officials who will best represent their interests. If representatives don't make laws the people like, they might not be reelected. Getting to have a say in making laws is a big **responsibility**.

CITIZENS IN ACTION

JAMES MADISON AND ALEXANDER HAMILTON WERE TWO OF OUR NATION'S FOUNDING FATHERS. THEY BELIEVED THE U.S. GOVERNMENT'S POWER SHOULD BE SPLIT UP INTO SEPARATE BRANCHES SO NO SINGLE PERSON WAS COMPLETELY IN CHARGE.

LEGISLATIVE

- MAKES LAWS
- APPROVES PRESIDENTIAL APPOINTMENTS
- TWO SENATORS FROM EACH STATE
- THE NUMBER OF CONGRESSMEN IS BASED ON POPULATION

EXECUTIVE

- SIGNS LAWS
- VETOES LAWS
- PARDONS PEOPLE
- APPOINTS FEDERAL JUDGES
- ELECTED EVERY FOUR YEARS

JUDICIAL

- DECIDES IF LAWS ARE CONSTITUTIONAL
- APPOINTED BY THE PRESIDENT
- THERE ARE 9 JUSTICES
- CAN OVERTURN RULINGS BY OTHER JUDGES

HAVING THREE BRANCHES OF GOVERNMENT CREATES A SYSTEM OF CHECKS AND BALANCES. THIS MEANS EACH BRANCH IS WATCHED BY THE OTHER BRANCHES SO NO BRANCH BECOMES TOO POWERFUL.

BREAKING RULES AND LAWS

When someone refuses to follow rules or laws, they may face **punishment**. Rules are often easier to break, so the consequences aren't as bad. When you break a rule at home or at school you might lose **privileges** or have to take a time-out.

Laws are more serious, so breaking them results in more serious consequences. People who break laws may have to pay fines or even spend time in jail. People who break laws may also have trouble getting jobs later in life.

IT'S NOT GOOD TO BREAK RULES OR LAWS, BUT BREAKING LAWS IS MUCH WORSE. YOU MAY LOSE PRIVILEGES, SUCH AS BEING ABLE TO DRIVE A CAR, OR YOU MIGHT BE SENT TO JAIL.

CITIZENS IN ACTION

DR. MARTIN LUTHER KING JR. WAS PUT IN JAIL SEVERAL TIMES FOR BREAKING LAWS WHILE FIGHTING FOR CIVIL RIGHTS. DR. KING BELIEVED SOME LAWS WERE UNJUST. BY BREAKING THEM, HE HOPED TO BRING ATTENTION TO THEM SO THEY WOULD BE CHANGED.

MAKING SOCIETY FAIR

Rules and laws make society a more fair and just place. Without them, the most powerful people would be able to make a society that was good for them but not for others.

Laws help make sure there are consequences for bad behavior, even for the most powerful people. We call this the rule of law. It means no single person is powerful enough to do anything they want, and it's one of the most important ideas in our nation.

THE RULE OF LAW IN THE UNITED STATES IS IN PART ESTABLISHED BY THE CONSTITUTION. THE CONSTITUTION CAN ONLY BE CHANGED BY LARGE MAJORITIES OF PEOPLE IN GOVERNMENT AND STATES VOTING TO MAKE A CHANGE.

MAKING SOCIETY FUNCTION

In addition to making society fair, rules and laws help society function, or work, better. Rules and laws make it clear to everyone what's expected of them. This means society is more predictable. With rules and laws, people can feel like they'll be able to go about their day without much trouble.

Think about how hard it would be to drive a car if there were no **traffic** laws. Drivers wouldn't stop for other cars, and there'd be car crashes all the time.

IF THERE WERE NO LAWS, PEOPLE MIGHT BE AFRAID TO DO THINGS SUCH AS CROSS THE STREET OR EVEN LEAVE THEIR HOME. RULES AND LAWS HELP SOCIETY RUN SMOOTHLY.

CHANGING RULES AND LAWS

Changing rules and laws can be hard, but it's not impossible. Imagine you have an early bedtime, but you want to stay up later. Your parents might change your bedtime if you can give them reasons why it'd be good for you to stay up.

To change a law, you need to **convince** your representatives to vote a certain way. You could also run for office yourself. It's easier to get rules and laws changed if you have good reasons for why things should be different.

ACTIVISTS BRING ATTENTION TO LAWS THEY'D LIKE TO SEE CHANGED. REPRESENTATIVES ARE MORE LIKELY TO VOTE TO CHANGE A LAW IF THEY KNOW THERE ARE LOTS OF PEOPLE IN FAVOR OF THE CHANGE.

GOOD REASONS FOR RULES AND LAWS

Rules and laws serve many purposes. They let people know what's expected of them. They also help society function better and be more fair for everyone. Laws may be difficult to make and change, but it's not impossible if citizens care deeply enough.

The next time your teacher or parent makes rules you don't like, take some time to think about them more carefully. They may have a purpose you didn't think of right away. They'll likely make your life better in the long run.

GLOSSARY

activist: Someone who acts strongly in support of or against an issue.

consequence: Something that happens as a result of a certain action or set of conditions.

Constitution: The document stating the basic laws by which the United States is governed.

convince: To make a person believe something.

encourage: To try to win over to a cause or action.

enforce: To make sure people do what is required by law.

predictable: Able to be known before happening.

privilege: A special right or favor.

punishment: The state of being made to suffer for wrongdoing.

represent: To act officially for someone or something.

responsibility: Something a person is in charge of.

serious: Deserving or involving a lot of attention, thought, or work.

traffic: The moving vehicles, such as cars and trucks, in a certain area.

INDEX

WEBSITES

Due to the changing nature of Internet links, PowerKids Press has developed an
online list of websites related to the subject of this book. This site is updated regularly.
Please use this link to access the list: www.powerkidslinks.com/civicv/rlpurp